SUCCESSION STORIES
from the FRONT LINE

INSIGHTS AND ADVICE *for*
CANADIAN BUSINESS OWNERS

D0974132

SARAH KRUGER *and* JAMES WONG

foreword by WILLIAM DOWNE

ISBN 978-0-9694357-1-6

Book Design by Fiona Raven
First Printing April 2008
Printed in Canada

Published by Bank of Montreal
1 First Canadian Place, 10th Floor
Toronto, Ontario M5X 1H3
1-866-886-0027
www.bmo.com/succession

The information in this publication is intended for general information only. It is not intended to be specific accounting, legal, tax, financial or other professional advice or recommendations for any individual or business. It may not be accurate, up to date or complete.

Readers are advised to seek appropriate accounting, legal, tax, financial and other professional advice in the applicable jurisdictions before acting or relying on any of the suggested strategies within this publication.

BMO Harris Private Banking, part of BMO Financial Group, provides an integrated wealth management approach to high net worth individuals and families. The private banking team of professionals is comprised of leading specialists in a variety of disciplines including banking, investment management, estate, trust and various family office services such as philanthropy and business succession planning.

CONTENTS

. . . . .

A MESSAGE FROM THE CEO

. . . . .

One of the biggest challenges facing many businesses in Canada is succession planning. Consider this: between 80 and 90 per cent of all companies in Canada are small to medium-size enterprises (SMES). They generate nearly half of the country's GDP and are responsible for some six million jobs. According to the Canadian Federation of Independent Business, seven out of ten SME owners intend to exit their businesses over the next ten years, yet only one-third of SME owners are currently planning for their eventual succession.

Lack of appropriate planning no doubt contributes to the fact that only one in three family businesses survives the transition to a second generation, and only one in ten the transition to a third. This represents a serious concern when so much of our economy depends on the viability and growth of this sector.

How do we explain the fact that so few of these companies survive into the second or third generation?

First, we know that independent business owners are "hands-on" managers. They tend to do everything themselves and are used to making all the important decisions. Of course, just like everyone else, independent business owners want to enjoy all the opportunities that life after retirement offers. However, the notion of letting someone else take over something so important and deeply personal as the family business can be hard to accept.

Another reason behind the apparent reluctance of business owners to prepare for their retirement is the lack of a frame of reference. After all, independent business owners know how to run their business, but often have nothing to guide them on the next step of handing it over to someone else.

There can be an opportunity cost to this situation. Without a well-crafted succession plan, a business can easily fail in the transition to the next generation. At the same time, having such a plan adds value to the company; if selling the business is the eventual outcome, this can increase its sale price.

At BMO, we have given a great deal of thought to ways we can help our customers deal with succession. We recognize that succession planning is part of a larger wealth management picture, and that a wide range of elements such as estate and trust planning, investment management and plans for philanthropy need to be considered.

While most independent business owners don't want some Bay Street banker to tell them what to do, I have been fortunate enough to have met with many such business owners from across the country. So, for what it's worth, here's the free advice I offer when we sit down together:

- While it can be hard to find the time, develop a succession plan while you are still actively involved in growing the business; talk to one of our experts – we can help.
- Avoid confusion; it can only lead to future confrontation.
- A good succession plan is the best way to ensure that your wishes are respected and that the business continues to grow and prosper.
- Read this book because it deals with succession issues in a very strategic way.
- Enjoy your retirement!

William Downe
President and CEO
BMO Financial Group

INTRODUCTION

. . . . .

This book is written for business families facing the challenge of planning the future of their businesses. What will happen when the current generation of owners and leaders decides to exit from the business?

In most successful businesses, great care is taken over important decision-making in an effort to prevent any possible risk of failure. However, business succession planning often does not receive the same dedicated attention, despite its importance to the overall survival of the business. Many reasons are given for this lack of attention – most relate to personal and emotional issues that families may be reluctant to even address, let alone share beyond their family confines. When this reluctance is coupled with an inability to deal with the complex business issues raised in succession planning, it is not surprising that the majority of Canadian business families are inadequately prepared for succession.

One way of overcoming the reluctance to discuss or share personal issues with non-family members is to understand there is little to be gained by trying to solve these problems in isolation. The reality is that many families face the same personal challenges and can draw comfort from sharing their situation and benefiting from a trusted advisor's experience in resolving succession issues.

The real life stories in this book were carefully chosen to highlight common challenges in succession planning and ways by which these problems might be addressed. How best to achieve good communication practices, the maintenance of family harmony, the timely grooming of successors and the management of sibling rivalry? Importantly, the stories also highlight the need for early planning and the need for a multidisciplinary approach to succession planning.

BMO Financial Group and BMO Harris Private Banking are keenly interested in the dynamics involved in the transition of the family business. Over a period of many years, we have worked with families and helped them transfer their businesses to the next generation of management and ownership. This book contains some of our accumulated knowledge and insights, as well as a framework to assist business families going through the succession planning process. For those business owners who have yet to get started, we believe these stories will provide both motivation and reassurance. Succession planning is a complex matter that requires objectivity, detailed thought, and open and honest communication with family and stakeholders. Once established, a commitment to continuing the planning process will serve families well for many generations to come.

Lastly, BMO Financial Group wishes to salute the Canadian families who have successfully transitioned their businesses – some of whom we have helped – and to encourage those families contemplating their transition to do so by fully engaging in the planning process with the help of their trusted advisors. In this way, business succession planning can serve as a unique opportunity to celebrate the achievements of the past and anticipate the promise of the future.

James Wong
Vice President Succession Planning
BMO Harris Private Banking

SOME FAMILIES SHARE THEIR STORIES

. . . . .

n the following chapters, several individuals have generously agreed to share their business succession experiences in order to benefit others faced with the same challenge. These experiences, some of which are painful or frustrating to recall, are all real; however, the names and types of businesses involved have been changed to respect the privacy of the families.

FERVENT DESIRES

. . . . .

Fred Olson is the third generation owner of a manufacturing business specializing in injection moldings for the automobile industry. The privately held firm has grown substantially from its beginnings as a small machine shop established by Fred's grandfather when he arrived in Ontario from Sweden. Fred enjoys recounting the ways in which each successive generation of his family has added value to the business. Personally, he would like the firm to retain its core business, but realizes that with changing business environments and markets, some degree of diversification will likely be necessary.

Fred married rather late in life and now, at age 59, has a son and a daughter who are still completing their education. His son has just finished his undergraduate studies; his daughter is pursuing a law degree. While his children are still at the stage of finding their way in the world, it is Fred's fondest wish that either one or both will assume an active role in the family business.

In Fred's case, succession planning may mean the appointment of an interim CEO in a mentorship position or even a diversification of the company's core business to better suit the interests of his children. He fervently wants the family enterprise to pass to the next generation and will undertake whatever steps are necessary to achieve this goal.

> *I was prompted into thinking about succession at a very young age because of my father. Ever since I can remember, he made it very clear that the business should always be kept in the family. His reasoning was that each succeeding generation could inherit the business, have the financial means to receive an education and ultimately have a place to work. The bottom line was that he saw business ownership as a way of ensuring that the family would always be financially independent.*

Fred has clearly embraced his father's philosophy and sees many other benefits accruing from ownership of a family-run business.

> *I think a family is much better off inheriting an operating business as opposed to an investment portfolio. The family is able to carry on its traditions in a tangible way and, as*

an owner, there's a certain amount of prestige involved. You receive respect from both the business community and the community at large. I enjoy being able to give back and I like to think my kids would too, as soon as they are in a position to do so.

Apart from these factors, I think there are sound economic reasons why business ownership makes sense. You're lucky if stocks and bonds grow more than 10 per cent per year, and there can be some very bad times that you can only hope will be balanced by the good years. Returns from a well-run business are much less susceptible to the ups and downs of the market. There are also tax advantages, and it's a lot easier borrowing money against an operating company.

Still, Fred is careful not to be too specific in his expectations.

In the future, I hope that my children will be actively involved in the business. However, both my son and daughter have to make a choice, at their own discretion, of what role they would like to play. I am proud to say that I never have, and never will, pressure them to take on a certain role within the organization. I'm pretty much open at this point to the various possibilities that the future may bring. It would obviously make it easier from a succession perspective to know what my children are planning but, at this time, I am being patient – waiting and watching how the children's involvement will evolve.

Fred looks back on his personal experience and is resolved to handle things differently with his own children.

My father took me under his wing from an early age and slowly taught me through having me work alongside him and observe how he did business. The problem with this method was that I didn't gain any confidence from working outside the business. I would have liked to become more independent by gaining experience in an unrelated field, possibly by working in a financial environment and learning about money. My lack of experience in this area meant that I had to catch up later while on the job. In general, I think I missed out on learning about people, experiences and decision-making on my own terms because my father wanted me to work alongside him. However, I have to say I did learn a lot about the different facets of the business and how my father reacted in certain situations. In later years when I was faced with similar situations, I knew how to react so, for the most part, I learned a lot from him.

I am taking a different approach in that my children will have the opportunity to work outside the business and develop core competencies that will enable them to become successful owners, regardless of their management function in the business.

The obvious challenge in Fred's succession planning is the significant age gap between himself and his children.

My biggest problem is that I have two children who are not yet ready to succeed me. My son is too young and inexperienced to be involved in the business at this time, and my daughter is not currently interested in being involved on a day-to-day basis. As a father, I ultimately want one, or both, of my children to succeed me. Unfortunately, this is not feasible at this time.

Since I am getting closer and closer to the age where I will want to step away from daily involvement in the business, I need to come up with an interim solution. With the help of my succession planning advisers, I am looking to hire a temporary Chief Executive Officer to help in the transition process to the kids.

This is essentially what happened when my father stepped down. Even though I had worked closely with him for some time, we both felt I was not yet ready to take on the leadership role. So we went out and found a retired CEO who was 65 and had extensive knowledge of the industry. We put the temporary CEO in control with the understanding that he would help transition the company to me.

Responsibilities and accountability were made clear to everyone from the beginning, so the relationship between the CEO and the family members involved went pretty smoothly. In general, I would have to say it's a good approach to take – the challenge will be to come up with the right individual for our current situation.

Of course, I'm not just concerned with filling the leadership position. I want to pass on a business that is well-managed at all levels, and to that end have been identifying possible candidates to succeed in various key positions.

Finding a suitable successor is just one aspect of transitioning a family business.

I've been working on my company's succession for the past five years, and it's not until you get into the nitty-gritty that you understand all of the eventualities. That's certainly one of the advantages of working with professionals – they can raise potential problems and present possible solutions that I might never have considered.

In my situation, I'm currently wrestling with the question of what to do if one of my children works for the company and the other does not. The way I see it, the one who works receives a salary and the challenge of running the business on top of the benefits accruing from ownership. However, I can see the possibility of that one child feeling that he or she is doing all the work while the other just sits back and receives the dividends. There doesn't seem to be an easy way around this problem.

While some issues are yet to be resolved, Fred and his family have made good progress handling other components of the succession planning process.

We have been having family meetings for the last three or four years – I'd have to say they've become an essential ingredient of the succession planning process. In family meetings, we discuss the "soft issues" of succession. So far, we've managed to come up with a shareholders' agreement, an employment policy and a mission statement. A big topic for us is developing conflict resolution mechanisms that everyone can agree to. I think you have to acknowledge that conflict is inevitable, so you need to figure out ways of managing it.

I'm pleased to see the children are also taking some initiative in attending meetings of the Board of Directors and being open to learning about the company and the possible ways in which it might evolve. I think there's a very good chance that one or both of them will play some kind

of significant role in the management of the company and –
who knows – may one day pass it on to their children.

WHAT THE ADVISERS SAY

Over the past several decades, a number of factors have created an "age gap" in the transitioning of family businesses. Couples have their children later in life, and young adults now typically take longer to complete their education or gain work experience outside the family firm. As well, outgoing owners are increasingly attracted to enjoying the benefits of early retirement. Consequently, many owners planning their exit strategies are finding their children are either too young or not yet ready to assume an ownership role.

Fred Olson's situation is certainly not unique. Fred does face an additional problem in that he is not certain whether either or both of his children will one day even wish to take an active role in the business. Despite his keen desire to keep the business within the family, Fred must prepare for a number of different scenarios and his planning must provide for a high degree of flexibility.

Fred's regular family meetings not only serve to educate his children, but also encourage an open discussion of possible alternative courses of action. It is also very commendable that the family has put in place a shareholders' agreement (one that contains provisions for having both active or inactive children as shareholders), an employment policy and a mission statement. But important work lies ahead to guarantee a smooth transition.

NEXT STEPS

- **Creation of a contingency plan**

  As a result of the age gap in Fred Olson's family situation, a contingency plan must be put in place to ensure continuity in the event of Fred's sudden death or illness. In many businesses, it is the Chief Operating Officer who steps in under these circumstances, but this outcome should not be left to chance. The situation should be considered ahead of time by dividing up the responsibilities, establishing time lines and agreeing on reporting procedures.

- **Creation of a successor development plan**

  Assuming that either one or both of the Olson children might eventually wish to take an active role in the business, it is important to plan the success of that future relationship. The plan should identify both the short and long-term goals of the successor(s) and outline suitable, necessary experience such as working outside the family business for a set period. The selection of a non-family mentor to support the successor(s) should also be an integral part of this plan.

- **Appointment of an interim CEO**

  As it may be years before either of Fred's children is ready to be CEO, Fred must start the interim candidate search process now. As part of selecting an appropriate interim CEO, clear boundaries and expectations need to be set for all parties. Working in a family-owned business presents a number of challenges for outside leaders, and it is important to plan ahead to minimize conflict and ensure a successful situation.

- **Planning for incapacity**

  Consideration should also be given to how voting shares are dealt with in the event of the owner's incapacity. A Voting Trust can give detailed direction and guidance to Trustees on how to vote shares in certain circumstances where the owner of those shares is incapable. Given the flexibility of Trusts, it can become easier over time to determine in whom, from among a possible group of successors, the voting shares shall ultimately be vested.

NO FREE RIDE

. . . . .

Marvin Renaud, a youthful 54-year-old with an athletic build, is a walking advertisement for his company's line of high-tech sports clothing. He hardly fits the stereotypical image of someone who spends a good portion of his time planning his retirement and yet that is exactly what he does, believing it to be essential to the future success and continuity of his business.

Marvin's privately held business was started by his grandfather and originally supplied apparel to the military during the Second World War. Marvin's father shifted the firm's focus toward supplying the emerging market for quality sports wear and, as the third-generation owner, Marvin has been quick to exploit the possibilities afforded by high-tech fabrics.

Marvin lives in the Montreal area where his manufacturing plant is located. He owns a string of specialty retail outlets that for some time were exclusive distributors of his product line. In recent years, however, an increasing portion of his sales has been generated online through the company's website.

Marvin is married and has two sons, aged 22 and 19. His older son has been working in the business for a little over a year; the younger is currently completing his university education. While Marvin is prepared to give his children the opportunity to take over the business, he is adamant that there will be "no free ride." Marvin expects his successor to earn the position through hard work.

I started in the business in 1981 and even though I was a late starter, my father put me through an A to Z apprenticeship. I tried my hand at every single thing, but this was probably due to my own sense of insecurity. I didn't want to be perceived as someone who was inexperienced. I had just come out of an unrelated post-graduate study program, I was recently married and I had no experience in the sportswear business, but I was pretty confident in myself. I spent a substantial amount of time serving my apprenticeship, but despite that I was able to buy out the company in 1994, only 13 years after I started. I had garnered the respect of the employees and had a good understanding of the business. By the time I bought out my father, I was probably one of the most experienced in the retail business in my area.

Never one to expect or ask for favours, Marvin engineered the buyout on his own initiative.

When I bought the business I took on quite a bit of debt. In my work I'd been exposed to senior people at the bank over the course of 10 years. I told my father I was interested in taking over the business, but he thought that I could never get the money together. Then I went over and met with the head of the bank with whom I had cultivated a relationship. I received the loan through an expansion of my line of credit and paid off the debt over a 10-year period.

Marvin appreciates the opportunity he was given to prove himself to his father and wants to give his own children a chance to succeed in the family business if they choose to take that path.

I feel that as a family business owner, I have the responsibility to at least give my children the opportunity to succeed me and take over the business. However, they would have to have the maturity, experience and motivation to buy me out.

Like most observers of the Canadian business scene, Marvin is keenly aware of the failure rate of many family businesses entering their third or fourth generation.

I don't believe in nepotism and I want the best for the well-being of the company and its employees. Therefore, senior and middle management know that I am giving my kids the opportunity to learn the business over the next decade, but there won't be a free ride. In 10 years, I will be 64 and I'd like to retire between 65 and 70. Whether my children will develop the necessary skills and means to buy me out by that time remains to be seen.

Part of Marvin's interest in a business succession plan comes out of a sense of responsibility to his employees.

I have always said my intention is that I want my business to go forward, with or without me. It's extremely demoralizing for employees when the succession planning is unclear, as there is the potential for them to get concerned about their well-being. It is a sensitive issue and because I am in a very cyclical business, I don't like to hire and fire people. I believe I have this moral contract with them. That being said, there will come a time when I will want to move on and enjoy the next stage of my life.

Marvin's commitment to the ongoing success of his company has made forward planning a priority.

I see people in similar situations to me who are much older and it can be quite difficult if they haven't planned accordingly. To dispose of a business, to plan a legacy program and to delegate enough to provide the experience for successors is very challenging. It can't be done at the last moment. I have already started building a legacy management program in terms of how to organize this business so that it's not a one-man show. These things take quite a bit of time, especially in my type of industry.

As most business owners know, it is hard to find the time to focus on succession when you are still running an operating business. However, in order to look at the whole picture, I realized I need to meet with succession planners, retirement planners and money managers, and I build these commitments into my schedule.

I think a lot of people deal with succession at the end, which is too late. When you are heavily involved in actively managing your business, people don't realize that it's a whole other issue to actually get out. Often it is difficult to exit when you leave it to the last minute and don't have a plan. That is a critical issue. It is one thing to talk about it, but it's another thing to execute.

Marvin is hoping that before long he will have a clearer idea of his sons' possible involvement in the company and then will be able to fill in the gaps in his planning.

> *I have a son currently working in the company's buying department, but in 10 years will he be able to run the whole business? When I started in the business, I was a workaholic and wanted to prove myself. But in my son's case, I think it's hard for him to garner the respect to move into other areas. He is good at what he does, but at this point he is limited to one facet of the business and can't do a wide variety of things due to a lack of formal education.*
>
> *My other son is at university. I feel I'm obliged to allow him to decide if he wants to be involved in the business as my father did the same for me. However, the day I finished my education, he asked me if I was going to be involved with the business so that he would know how to plan accordingly. Similarly, I feel a need to know if my sons are going to come in and if they are, will they do a staged entry to assess if they have the skill sets? And, if they do have the skills, they still need the financial resources to get some sort of capital to buy me out. I am not going to give them the business, that's for sure.*

Given the complexities of today's business world, Marvin is keenly aware that the business cannot be carried forward on the basis of his sons' efforts alone.

If one of my sons becomes the owner, he will need a number of experienced senior and mid-level executives. The ones I have had so far are people that I hired from within and actually, at the time, I didn't need very sophisticated people. However, today's retail arena is a very aggressive environment that requires experienced managers.

In terms of business operations and the required learning curve, it is not that easy to find someone to replace the CEO, whether on an interim or permanent basis. I am currently looking outside, but I would prefer to look within. My industry is not necessarily attractive to executives with the right skill sets. At one time, I was the innovator and I was able to plan what steps had to be taken, and the other managers were executors. What it takes to be a CEO is to know about many aspects of the business, to know how to manage many different managerial issues, and this is what I'm trying to impress on my family members.

Whatever the eventual ownership will be, it is clear that Marvin wants the business to succeed along the lines that he, his father and grandfather have worked so hard to establish.

One of my greatest fears would be for the company to be bought by someone looking to fire people and completely change the culture. In terms of my children succeeding me,

I think that they get along very well and collectively have the ability to occupy different key and mutually exclusive roles in the business. The real issue is, do they have the diversity of skill sets that will benefit the company or will they be a financial drain if, for example, they want to be passive owners rather than active managers? That's the big question.

Looking to the future, Marvin is not distracted by the uncertainties over which he has no control.

I quite clearly look at what the business needs. Regardless of whether my family comes in, the company needs to prepare for my eventual retirement. I am preparing the firm structurally so that by the time I leave there will be more modern business processes, both organizational and managerial. As a legacy, I want to leave a company that is highly cost-efficient rather then being simply profitable from the net retail or gross profit point of view.

The company and the legacy program need to be more structured, with or without my sons' involvement. I always tell my employees that the day I become an impediment, I will not hesitate to bring someone in from the outside. In the meantime, I am here because I love my job and I love what I do.

WHAT THE ADVISERS SAY

Marvin demonstrates a remarkable ability for putting the business and its needs first. Unlike many owners engaged in the process of succession planning, he is not prepared to allow his vision for the future of his business to be clouded by the type of family issues that typically take centre stage.

Although he is at least 10 years away from his projected retirement date, Marvin is already fully engaged in succession planning. To increase the odds of a successful transition, he is involving all his key advisers – bankers, lawyers, accountants and retirement planners – in an integrated team approach. This strategy saves time and also reduces the likelihood of anything being overlooked.

Only time will tell whether Marvin's children are up to the task of running the company, but if they do assume a leadership position, there is no doubt they will have earned the right to do so. In the meantime, Marvin is keeping his employees informed regarding his retirement intentions and is concentrating his efforts on building a strong management team.

Nepotism, real or perceived, can be a problem in the family business transition. Fear of being seen as the "favoured child" can deter some potential successors. Even if allegations of nepotism are not made, successors may be compared to the previous generation and have their credibility questioned. Providing the successor with a neutral third person with whom to discuss these matters can be very helpful.

NEXT STEPS

- **Creating an exit plan**

  With the help of his advisers, Marvin can now create a timeline for both his short- and long-term goals so that the real planning can begin. Once an exit time frame is established, it is easier to determine the specific needs of the business and how the departing owner can help to ensure a smooth transition. Businesses have a much higher success rate when there is either a phased buyout or a phased management transition. When exiting leaders work with their successors, the transfer of both skills and the transition of the business culture are more effective.

- **Creating a tax-efficient transition**

  It is important that Marvin's transition is tax efficient. Often a Trust is used to expand the number of taxpayers who can access Capital Gains Exemptions available while maintaining control, assuming the business qualifies for the exemption. A Trust can also mitigate the taxes payable on Marvin's eventual exit. In addition, a Discretionary Family Trust holding voting shares allows for flexibility by buying time to see who emerges as the best leader from within the family.

- **Establishing a business valuation**

  The estimated fair market value of the business is an important input to Marvin's financial planning and forms the financial basis for ownership transition. Understanding the elements that drive business value will help Marvin to focus on planning his exit. As the valuation is needed primarily for planning purposes, it does not need to be in elaborate detail. A simple estimated value range will often suffice. Should Marvin in the future contemplate a family transition, then a fully supported valuation will be required to ensure compliance with tax regulations.

- **Planning for retirement**
  Marvin has worked hard and is quite rightly looking forward to his retirement. He knows that a happy and rewarding retirement requires considerable thought and planning. Given the personality of Marvin – a determined, intelligent, driven entrepreneur – one cannot imagine him going from running a multi-million dollar business to sitting by the pool. Many business owners make the mistake of thinking that all they want to do is play golf when they retire but then, within three months, they are back in the office. It is important for people like Marvin to set personal goals for retirement and plan ahead to satisfy their success-oriented personalities.

ON THEIR OWN TERMS

· · · · ·

Brenda Kolecki's grandfather was a pioneer in the early development of the Alberta oil industry. Following the LeDuc discovery in 1947, a number of fledgling companies quickly sprang up to service the needs of explorers and producers alike. Brenda's grandfather became an early leader in the field by purchasing and amalgamating three such companies, establishing a headquarters in Calgary.

In 1977, Brenda's father and uncle took over the business. They operated as equals in the decision-making process, although Brenda's father was the company's public face.

In 2001, Brenda and her cousin Thomas, both in their early forties, became CEO and President respectively. This occurred largely as a result of both their fathers wanting their children to assume the role of president. Unfortunately, the co-presidency arrangement proved untenable, and the two cousins now seek a more suitable partnership.

My father started in the business when he was 17 and served an apprenticeship by working from the ground up. My uncle, on the other hand, took a different route and went to university and then worked for another firm before joining the business. Everything went well for a number of years, but by the late 1970s some disagreement arose between my Dad and my grandfather about the direction of the company. My Dad, who was a vice-president at the time, was getting frustrated enough that he considered leaving the business. After my grandmother's intervention, my grandfather agreed to talk things out and try to understand my father's perspective. The upshot was that my grandfather decided to leave for a year and see how his two sons would handle the business in his absence. This wasn't too difficult for him to do since he had a very full life outside the business with fishing and golf. When my grandfather came back a year later, he was satisfied with how the company was operating so they all decided to put a deal in place that would allow my uncle and father to buy him out.

Brenda's father put a fair bit of pressure on her to come into the business. He was aware of her interests and showed her ways in which they could be related to the family firm.

I received my Bachelor's degree in Arts and my Master's

degree in Philosophy and I had no intention of working in business, family-owned or otherwise. But I also didn't have any idea of what I wanted to do. My Dad knew I was very idealistic, but he thought I could achieve at least some of my goals by working in the family company. What he impressed on me was that a business could improve people's lives. As a business owner he felt responsible for his 300 employees and their families – something he found both challenging and rewarding.

My experience working at our company was as an accounting assistant, and I did it part time as I finished up my degree. Somewhat to my surprise, I found I really liked working for the family firm. When I finished school, my Dad suggested an interview with our Vice-President of Marketing since Dad felt the best role for me would be in that area. I was still quite ambivalent about the possibility of working at the company or elsewhere. I really didn't know what I wanted to do and I didn't pursue other options – I simply took my Dad's advice. The person who interviewed me was able to relate to me and my political interests. He was able to talk about how he'd managed to achieve his goals while working in a corporate environment.

Having become more predisposed to working for the family firm, the idea of assuming an ownership role began to grow on Brenda.

For five years I worked in marketing, and I also had customer service projects, recruiting assignments and was part of a quality advisory team. Then we purchased a company in Edmonton in 1998, and it was decided that I should run it as a subsidiary. This marked the beginning of our family starting the succession process. We used our trusted adviser as a facilitator, and he helped us every step of the way. We had individual interviews and discussed strategic planning and so on. Both Tom and I have siblings who are involved in the business, but not in an ownership position so it was important to involve them in the process as well.

My Dad and uncle were keen to see the family firm managed by the next generation. We didn't come up with anything as grandiose as a family vision – it was just assumed that my cousin and I would take over, and that we would work out the details from there. At this point, I was in Edmonton running a subsidiary with 40 employees and my cousin Tom was working on his Master's degree in Business Administration.

Brenda's father and uncle were careful to ensure that the company's management team was kept fully informed and engaged in the succession planning process.

One thing that became very important to us was to involve

the non-family executives so that they would become comfortable with our positions in the company. My cousin and I needed to show leadership, and there was no better way than to work with the executive and middle-management team to develop the company's goals. Around this time, our Vice President of Corporate Development was putting together a five-year plan for the business, and we took that on as our vision and fit the pieces together accordingly.

By 2002, the business had officially made the transition to the next generation.

My uncle and Dad were still active, but the ownership had officially transferred from second generation brothers to third generation cousins. Tom and I became equal owners and managing leaders. From the employees' perspective, though, everyone still felt that our fathers were running the show. This didn't bother us at all. We really enjoyed having our fathers around for the transition as we were able to benefit from their experience and learn from them at a comfortable distance.

We had originally thought the succession process would take about 10 years, but instead it happened in about five years. I think my cousin and I attribute that to the fact we were able to seize our opportunity and leverage our skills into becoming successful owners.

The period of mentorship unfortunately came to an end with the deaths of both Brenda's father and uncle.

The company was evaluated in 2001. Now, instead of the original buyout provisions, we are redeeming the value of our fathers' shares to their estates. My mother and aunt are beneficiaries of the estates and, in a sense, the estates retain control of the company, but there has been no interference whatsoever. The role our mothers play is pretty much what it has always been, which is to be informed but not involved in operational decisions.

Wishing to honour their fathers' wishes, Brenda and her cousin spent six years operating the company as co-leaders.

When we took ownership in 2001, we followed the co-leader model with the titles, President and CEO. In our case, this model was a concession to our fathers. Both of our fathers wanted us in the presidency role and, in turn, Tom and I had to figure out what it meant for us to follow that type of model. There was no formalizing of our responsibilities or tools to measure our success in our respective functions. It was more or less understood that Tom would be on the operations side where he was already working, and that I would be on the sales and marketing side.

The co-leader model ultimately proved to be unworkable, and now Brenda and Tom are working to redefine their separate roles.

For six years we gave the co-leader model a really good shot but, almost from the beginning, having to report to each other on a daily basis was a huge problem and created a lot of friction. In terms of conflict resolution, we knew instinctively that seeking our Dads' advice was not necessarily the best direction to go. Instead, we chose to have our conflict mediated by the same trusted adviser who had facilitated our succession. What was nice about the facilitator was that he knew all of us very well and eventually he helped us understand that the co-leader structure wasn't making the best use of our time or the company's time. I think Tom and I both knew that if we weren't efficient at making decisions together then, more importantly, we could hardly expect our management to be efficient. Part of the arrangement that we came up with was that Tom would be the president and would be responsible for the day-to-day management and execution. I, in return, am focusing on long term business and corporate development. In addition, as owners and managers there was a lot of informality in how we operate, and we are working on correcting this by spelling out our responsibilities more clearly.

Fortunately for Brenda and Tom, the conflict over their opera-tional roles did not compromise their personal relationship.

We are lucky in our family in that there is a lot of common sense, a lot of emotional maturity and a desire on everyone's part to see the business succeed. My cousin and I always real-ized that we had to preserve our family relationship. When we were coping with our partnership problems and deciding on an optimal way of doing things, we realized there are times when you have to balance the business and the family, and at times it isn't always possible to put the business first. The interconnected nature of family businesses makes it dif-ficult to draw the lines. It becomes a constant balancing act. I think that putting the business first is an ideal, but it is dif-ficult to always put it first.

Even though Brenda and her cousin have been able to settle their differences amicably, she does acknowledge the need to have their professional relationship established in a more formal-ized manner.

We don't have an exit strategy in our shareholders' agree-ment, and I admit that does scare me a bit. We were once an informal company that was led by common sense, and now we are slowly moving towards more formality and documentation. We are still engaged in that process, but working through it has helped us understand our separate objectives. As of now, our shareholders' agreement does not take into account certain key areas like exit options; it basically just covers a code of conduct. I think it is important for us to also consider certain soft issues like spouses' involvement and ownership rules.

At this point, Brenda is not only seeking a new role for herself, but is also re-examining her original commitment to continuing her father's legacy.

Since my father passed away, I have been doing a lot of soul searching. I am certainly feeling the pressure of continuing my father's legacy. Part of the problem is that I just sort of drifted into the business, and now I'm questioning how much I've been doing for me and how much was to please my father. Before my father passed away, I started talking to him about a possible role change. I really dreaded having to do it because I knew my father would be completely opposed. He was of the firm belief that my cousin and I should represent the family equally and as co-leaders.

I've always felt the need to please my father and I know that stepping down as president would have disappointed him. On the other hand, no one forced me to step down. It was my decision. I firmly believed we were not operating our business to its full potential and so I took the necessary action. Ironically, my father's death can be credited with helping me become strong enough to make that sort of decision.

Looking back, there are several aspects of her career development that Brenda wishes she had handled differently.

Because of my lack of formal training in business, I think it took me a lot longer than the average person to feel comfortable with my position as a business executive. Also, I think it is necessary to have a certain level of technical knowledge in finance. Perhaps most importantly, I strongly believe I would have benefited from outside work experience in a related industry. For example, it would have illustrated to me that our way is not the only way. It would have made me realize, sooner rather than later, that I didn't have to be my Dad and that there are different types of success and different ways of becoming successful. My father was unconditionally supportive, but it is often more meaningful to hear positive feedback from an unbiased source, which is what I missed out on from not working elsewhere.

Looking ahead, Brenda is optimistic about the future prospects for the company. At the same time, she continues to struggle to find an appropriate focus for her skills.

I have now stepped into the role of being an owner and not a manager. Organizationally, everyone reports to Tom, and I don't have a day-to-day role anymore. I think my stepping down as president was a great decision for the company. Tom has the drive and ambition to be the president, and I feel he is better suited than I am for the leadership role.

I am focusing more on long-term strategic planning and keeping the agenda alive. This is something that's easier to do when you are not focused on day-to-day operational issues. I am also in the process of researching possible candidates for a board of advisers whose purpose would be strategy creation and review. I'm not sure what other roles the future will hold for me, personally, but time will tell.

I think that our company is going through a renewal now. We are continuing the legacy, but on our own terms. By doing so, we are taking the company in a new and exciting direction – one that our fathers might never have imagined.

WHAT THE ADVISERS SAY

Brenda Kolecki offers us insights into the succession process from the unique perspective of the successor – the person charged with the responsibility of moving forward under conditions that are sometimes less than ideal.

In Brenda's case, for example, her father pressured her to join the firm at a young age instead of encouraging her to broaden her education (unlike her cousin Tom) or gain outside work experience. Now, Brenda feels insufficiently prepared to be in a top management position. Without education in finance, human resources, sales, marketing and negotiation, successors are at a distinct disadvantage. Thus, encouraging education and outside work experience for potential successors can be the key to effective succession planning.

As successors, Brenda and Tom adopted a management model that was a concession to their fathers. Co-leadership is never easy and requires a commitment to creating an efficient process by which to manage the business. Although there are ways to structure co-ownership and control to ensure that it is equitable, Brenda and Tom experienced frustration and conflict using the co-leadership model and could certainly have benefited from a clearer definition of their roles and responsibilities. Fortunately, Brenda and Tom had sufficient common sense and emotional maturity to handle the challenge.

Brenda and Tom were wise to work with the non-family executives to develop goals for the company. They gained respect and credibility in the process. However, since their fathers remained active in the firm despite having officially relinquished ownership, it was some time before the employees perceived the cousins to be the leaders of the company.

At this point, Tom and Brenda are demonstrating an ability to move on from the situation they inherited and, with the help of advisers, to continue the legacy on their own terms.

NEXT STEPS

- **Development of an advisory board**

  The appointment of an advisory board should be a high priority for Brenda and Tom, and she has already begun the work of identifying potential candidates. A well-chosen advisory board will provide a buffer between the two families and assist in conflict mediation. An advisory board will also serve as neutral territory for the discussion of governance, family issues and strategic planning. Many people underestimate the benefit of having an advisory board and mistakenly assume that it serves a similar function as a corporate board. In fact, an external advisory board is oriented towards providing objectivity and serving the best interests of the families *and* the business, rather than focusing solely on the needs of the business.

- **Delineation of roles**

  Brenda has recently made the transition from the day-to-day involvement of being president to a less well-defined role in long-term strategic planning – "keeping the agenda alive," as she puts it. She is in an uncertain position of working in the business, but not having a management position. Even though her role is still evolving, at some point it would be beneficial for Brenda and Tom to sit down with their advisers to define their individual functions and establish mutual expectations. The advisory board will serve them well as impartial observers of their respective accountability.

- **Review of the shareholders' agreement**
  Despite having an amicable working arrangement, Brenda and Tom need to review their shareholders' agreement, for their own protection and that of the business. To date, they have demonstrated an admirable ability to handle potentially divisive situations, but this may not always be possible. Every family business needs a strong shareholders' agreement clearly outlining a conflict resolution mechanism, with either a shotgun clause or auction process in place.

- **Addition of a business valuation clause**
  Despite the current co-ownership, at some point Brenda and Tom could consider adding an objective business valuation mechanism to their shareholders' agreement. A pre-agreed valuation formula may be simple to draw up, but since it cannot anticipate every possible change in the economic circumstances of the

business, unnecessary conflict can result. Personal differences can be minimized by adding a clause in the agreement allowing each party to prepare a valuation and establishing a mutually agreeable process for review.

BEST LAID PLANS

. . . . .

ord Walker was once the heir apparent to a successful family enterprise – a marina and string of related businesses operating on the west coast of B.C. As the only son in a family of five, it was assumed that Gord, now 46, would carry on the family business into a second generation.

Retirement planning by Gord's father included hiring a facilitator to guide the family through succession issues. This proved to be a challenging but necessary experience, and the family was finally able to establish a workable shareholders' agreement. For a time, the business was run effectively with a board of advisers working in a mediating capacity.

Ultimately, competitive forces proved too strong for the family-run business, and the decision was made to sell. Gord's company became just another statistic: only one in three small and medium-sized businesses survive the transition to a second generation, and only one in ten survive the transition to a third generation.

Although the Walker family was ultimately unable to keep the marina, the lessons learned are currently more valuable than ever. On behalf of his family, Gord now manages the wealth that was realized on the sale of the business and is already planning the transfer of these assets to the next generation.

I was the only boy in a family of five and, as a result, I think I received a tremendous amount of favouritism. My perception from a young age was that I would be the heir apparent, but my father was very concerned about the whole nepotism issue. Through summer jobs at the marina, I was given challenging work experience – starting at the bottom and working my way up. I always tried to live up to my father's expectations – there was certainly a fair bit of pressure that way. As a young man, I wasn't certain whether or not I wanted to work for the family firm. So I worked for a while outside the business, and then I did a business degree. Eventually, I started my own little company, which was a great confidence-boosting experience. I very much wanted to do something on my own and prove my mettle both to my father and me.

After taking the time to pursue other options, Gord Walker finally made the decision to join the family firm.

The process of joining the company came about from approaching my father and saying I wanted to take over the business. He was receptive, but made it abundantly clear he expected nothing but the best in terms of my work perform-ance. When I look back, I see him as a hard taskmaster, but he also had an incredible ability to develop people's skills. He would give me areas of responsibility that were outside my comfort zone, and I ended up doing jobs that I never dreamed I'd have the ability to do. In retrospect, I see there was definitely planning and astuteness on my father's part during the transition process.

As a result of his father's mentorship, Gord grew more confident in taking a leadership role.

Gradually, I gained more control of the business. My Dad and his managers were all approaching retirement so it just became natural for me to take on more of the day-to-day work and decision-making. I was able to develop my own management team and that made me feel more in charge.

As the retirement of Gord's father grew closer, the need to agree on a written succession plan became more pressing.

By this time, one of my sisters had assumed responsibility for human resources in the business, and my father felt that the two of us would own shares in the business and that our three other sisters would own the company's real estate. At that time, the real estate and the business were more or less of equal value. However, he came to realize that this approach was going to be problematic – apart from the realization that real estate can fluctuate in value, there was also the fact that the real estate holdings were tied so closely to the operation of the business.

My father came to the conclusion that it would be more fair and effective if all five children became shareholders in the combined assets of the firm and the real estate. A facilitator was hired to guide us through this process.

Gord was unprepared for the many personal and emotional issues that arose during the transitioning process.

During our family meetings with the facilitator, I was totally taken aback by the resentment that was expressed towards me by my sisters. Growing up, I suppose it's only natural that you develop some sibling rivalries, but my parents had instilled strong values in us such as, family always comes first and that family unity is very important. Even though I think we all shared those values, the reality was that I was the only son, and my sisters felt a lot of resentment. I had been totally oblivious to these issues, and I was shocked at some of the stuff that came out. For example, my sister who was involved in the business had some issues with the fact that I was appointed to the leadership role and that she was not given that same opportunity. There were many issues that we had to deal with as a family.

At this point, we learned about the whole concept of family councils. With the help of our legal team, we drafted the shareholders' agreement that included such issues as how we would conduct ourselves, what decisions would require unanimous support and what decisions would not. We also had a buy/sell agreement so that anyone could exit the business. The process of working with the family facilitators was painful and a real eye-opener, but it was essential to get all the ground rules in place.

As time went on, it became apparent that the shareholders' agreement, as originally drafted, created problems in the day-to-day running of the operation.

My father really wrestled with some of his succession planning decisions. Towards the end, he also changed his mind a lot about his estate planning decisions. I think he was under the misconception that fair means equal but, in reality, equal doesn't always mean fair. By giving all of us shareholders an equal voice, he made it very hard for me to be in charge. In the context of running a business, the last thing you need to worry about is having to ask non-active owners what they think about every little decision. Being micromanaged did not work very well from either a strategic or personal perspective. Under the terms of our shareholders' agreement, I didn't have effective control.

In the end, we agreed that the original shareholders' agreement wasn't working, and we amended it to include a board of advisers selected by an executive recruiter. We wanted individuals with strategic, logistical and marketing skills. We purposely stayed away from my Dad's friends, and hired people with strong backgrounds who were impartial. We interviewed and chose the members of the advisory board. Probably the reason why our board was so successful was because we went through the process of creating it together. Therefore, the board was viewed as impartial.

The appointment of an advisory board made a significant difference to the way Gord was able to run the business.

Having an outside group of advisers broadened my perspective and provided valuable feedback. I have to say that growing up in a family business, I had been sheltered in a way from outside criticism, and that's not always a good

thing. The board also offered opportunities from a net-
working perspective. Perhaps most importantly, the board
provided a buffer between my sisters and me. They knew
that the advisory board had to approve my plans and make
decisions based on our family's collective best interests. They
got the peace of mind that it wasn't just their little brother
calling the shots and doing whatever he wanted, willy-nilly.
It also worked well from a communications point of view.
The chair of the advisory board would report back to the
other shareholders and explain what was going on. The
chair and my sisters definitely still had input, but it was in
a more organized and civil manner. Essentially, we relied
on the buffer of the advisory board as our conflict resolu-
tion plan.

Despite the success of the new working arrangement, the family
business was confronted by other pressing challenges.

Eventually, we got strategically caught in a no man's land.
The competition moved into our market area, and we didn't
think we could compete with the big players. With the writ-
ing on the wall, we had a family conference and decided
we would sell rather than try to hang on and end up losing
money. It was agreed that we'd enter a strategic partnership
with our competitor – a move that we all regretted to some

degree, especially my Dad, but we made the decision that was best for us as a family.

Surrendering control of the business meant a new, diminished, role for Gord.

It was a novel and very different experience for me to work for someone else. I did it for three years, and I have to say that was the worst period in my life. Basically, I came from a family business environment where I could walk right into my father's office and discuss an issue with him and come up with a solution. In my new role, I had to prove myself in a manner that I was unaccustomed to—and it became frustrating.

Essentially, when we entered into the strategic partnership they were the "dog" and we were the "tail." They owned 77 per cent and we owned 23 per cent of the combined company. Despite their majority control, the fact remained that I had grown up on the West coast and was making decisions based on my experience with that market. These individuals had no knowledge of our local situation, which is why we had formed the partnership in the first place.

Essentially, I spent three years defending my management, our strategy and our positioning, and I really resented it, although I can't say I wasn't warned. I can remember one of my advisory board members telling me when we made the sale that: "Those people will be monitoring you. You are going to be working for them, and they are going to want value out of their acquisition. You're going to have to make real change and be able to drive the numbers they want."

When it came right down to it, I had so much trouble trying to drive the numbers versus running the company the way my father had. All of the other family members involved in the business felt the same frustration. The purchaser just didn't have the same mentality as a family business: we had a different set of values and goals for our business.

Gord and his family were faced with making another difficult decision.

It could have been a very divisive situation, but in the end I think we all concluded that since the business could no longer be run as my father would have wished, we'd be better off selling. We sold our shares to the majority shareholder, and that was the end of our involvement in running a marina. Ironically, our father passed away right at this time. All of a sudden, we received our financial legacy and experienced this new-found wealth. Prior to the sale, the wealth had all been tied up in the business.

By this time, Gord and his sisters were accustomed to using family meetings as a forum for important decision-making.

I got together with my sisters, and we looked around the table. We really didn't know what to do. After a series of meetings, we decided to form a holding company together.

I think there were a number of reasons why we ended up staying together: we are a close-knit family, our parents instilled strong family values in us, we knew our parents would have wanted us to stay together and, quite honestly, we didn't know what else to do. None of us were raised thinking we'd one day have to manage a substantial amount of wealth.

No longer involved in running a marina, Gord has now assumed a new role managing the family's assets.

My new role is basically to preserve our family's capital, and that presents challenges of a different kind. Once we'd made a conscious decision to stick together as a family, I knew that my sisters were putting their faith and trust in my skills. There is an extraordinary amount of pressure on me to meet their expectations regarding our family's legacy.

In establishing the holding company, I was insistent that we all meet with our lawyers, accountants and bankers. There are just so many aspects to consider. We kept on our original Chief Financial Officer from the family business, and he is now responsible for managing the family office and our investments.

I have noticed a change in my sisters now that we are dealing with a portfolio of financial assets. I think it feels more real to them, and they are taking more of an interest and more of an active role in managing their money while still trusting me to make the important decisions. We have monthly shareholder meetings and have our CFO walk us through our investments. We are constantly learning.

Gord and his sisters are gradually adjusting to the benefits and responsibilities that have come with their new-found wealth. Now, their concern is for the future.

At this stage in our planning, we, as shareholders, are trying to assess if, how and when we are going to pass on our assets to the next generation. We want to educate our children. Personally, I want my children to find their own path in life. It's important that they define who they are and what they want to be. I want them to follow their passions rather than living off their inheritance. Some words my father passed on to me have resonated strongly in my life: "I could be a lot bigger than I am today, but every morning I look in the mirror and I'm happy with the person I see."

WHAT THE ADVISERS SAY

Throughout their business succession, Gord and his sisters never lost sight of their primary goal – to keep their family relationships close and intact. The decision to sell a family business is never easy, but here it was jointly decided, and a divisive situation was avoided. Since the business could no longer be run in accordance with the family's shared values, it was time to let it go. The Walker family did what was right for them and, in the process, managed to preserve significant wealth. The experience gained from operating a business together is now serving them well in managing the assets they realized on the sale of the marina.

The establishment of a board of advisers was the best thing the Walker family could have done, for their business and also for family unity. Gord, being the heir apparent, was faced with tremendous pressure to operate the business on a profitable footing. In addition, Gord's four sisters harboured some resentment of Gord's privileged position. The advisory board served as a much-needed buffer between the active and inactive shareholders in the Walker family.

Gord's succession experience demonstrates the importance of looking ahead and putting procedures in place that can handle any number of possible outcomes. Taking this lesson to heart, Gord and his siblings are already considering how they will successfully manage to transfer their wealth and family values to their children.

NEXT STEPS

- **Education of the next generation**

  While the Walker family is now dealing with an investment port-folio rather than a business, there is still a sense that the shared wealth is the embodiment of the work and values of previous generations. The family is already thinking about the impact of this family legacy on the next generation. They wish to prevent their children from simply choosing to live off their inheritance rather than finding their own way in the world. One suggestion for the Walker family is to hold family meetings to begin educating the next generation on family values, and to start exploring a vision for the management of the inherited family wealth in addition to developing financial fluency skills.

- **Creation of a private foundation**

  Another suggestion for the Walkers would be to create a private foundation that would not only consolidate the family's philan-thropic initiatives, but would also give the third generation the opportunity to work together on a worthwhile endeavour. Such a foundation could be extremely useful as a means of instilling a work ethic and acting as a vehicle for transferring family values from one generation to the next.

- **Review of agreements**

  Through the upheaval of the last few years, the Walker family has been very successful in finding ways to avoid potential conflict by putting the appropriate governance procedures and legal agreements in place. A periodic review of these arrangements to ensure they are still fulfilling their original intent is advisable. For example, now that the Walkers are using a family office as a base from which to manage their portfolio, new issues may arise that will need to be addressed such as whether it is appropriate for shareholders to expect office support staff to handle their personal correspondence. An agreement defining such matters will avoid petty squabbles.

Changes in family members' circumstances or a change in the investment strategy of the portfolio may also result in a need to review core documents such as the holding company's shareholders' agreement. Would a transition to less liquid investments still accommodate a family member's sudden need to exit?

A family is not a static entity and periodic reviews of governance procedures are essential to continuing good relations.

DIVIDE AND CONQUER

· · · · ·

Fraser McFarlane grew up as the middle son of three boys – all in line to become the third generation to run their grandfather's business. From modest beginnings in Nova Scotia and New Brunswick, the company had grown to become one of Canada's largest producers of manufactured wood products with production facilities in five provinces.

Fraser's father was CEO for more than 30 years and found it difficult to address the issue of succession planning. Contemplating his own exit from the company was clearly a painful process for him. Eventually, a consultant was retained to facilitate the transitioning to the three boys, all of whom were working in the business. But, unfortunately, Fraser's father rejected all the work that had been done. This provoked a family crisis and ultimately a situation in which the board of directors forced out Fraser and his younger brother under somewhat Machiavellian circumstances.

Now, in his early sixties, Fraser is able to look back on his experience with a certain degree of calm and equanimity. He has prospered in his new career, is happy to be free of the pressures of running the family business and enjoys the time he can now spend with his wife and children. His story, however, is a salutary reminder of the ways in which succession planning can go bad, leaving families permanently scarred by unresolved conflict.

Growing up, our dinner table conversations always seemed to revolve around what was happening in the business. My two brothers and I were encouraged to visit our father at work and over time we became friendly with many of the executives.

I went to business school and got my Master's in Business Administration and when I finished school, I was offered a job at Goldman Sachs. However, my father came to me and told me he felt I had an obligation to the family to work in the business for a minimum of three years. Being the dutiful son, I complied.

Like most potential successors, Fraser was exposed to many aspects of the firm's operations.

I was moved around a lot at the beginning because our company had operations across Canada. I moved up through the ranks by going through the various positions. Cyclicality affects every business, but when I got to a senior management level it was at a time when sales started to go up. That reflected well on me, and I ended up running the western region. Then I came back east and, 20 years after I joined the firm, I was appointed president.

As Fraser was working his way up in the organization, his two brothers were also part of the business.

I always had more senior positions. My older brother, Alex, was terrific socially and did a great job representing the business. He was very good being the face of the company, but he didn't have a business background and therefore didn't have an appreciation for business issues. Alex would have been an excellent chairman. My younger brother, Ian, and I both had an MBA, and we both saw eye-to-eye strategically and operationally. We would get together and have a lot of fun socially. We really saw things the same way, but Alex would often have a totally different perspective.

Despite their different roles, all three brothers were equal shareholders.

My brothers and I all had an equal interest in the business, but we had difficulty agreeing on the roles that each of us would have. I was not at all sure that I would be comfortable in the role of president forever. My father was still active by his CEO title, but not operationally.

Uncertainty over the transitioning of the business added a great deal of strain to the day-to-day running of the firm.

My father was not prepared to deal with succession. He had a kind of wait-and-see attitude. Mostly, I think, his hesitation came from an unwillingness to ever formally surrender the reins even though he already had, for all practical purposes.

Over the years, frustration built up over trying to get our father to look at the succession issue more formally. We had used a major consulting firm for a number of high-level strategic issues, and my father had known the adviser very well. We all thought these contacts could be the means of getting the ball rolling. However, the adviser was not interested in working with me alone because he wanted us to come forth unanimously as a family in deciding to hire a consultant. To me this was kind of a telling statement and certainly pointed to the trouble that lay in store for us as a family. In the end, we found an adviser who met with us on a monthly basis for a year. In many family businesses, there is a desire not to let outsiders in on what's happening within the family but, in our case, it was necessary to let someone in. Left to our own devices, we never would have come up with a plan.

Working with the adviser turned out to be an eye-opening experience.

Our adviser worked with my two brothers and me on an individual basis. He asked a lot of tough questions: "What's happening in the world," "What are the big issues we should be looking at," "What's happening in the company," "What are our strengths and weaknesses," "What should we be doing strategically to grow the business," "What parts of the business should be there and what shouldn't" and, finally, "How do you personally fit into the organizational structure?" There were huge differences in the way my brothers and I saw the world, the business and our roles in the company. Somehow, we came up with a reasonable agreement regarding our organizational structure: my older brother would be Chairman, I would be Chief Executive Officer and my younger brother would be Executive Vice President. I wouldn't say we were totally unanimous about every detail, but we were pretty close. Ian realized that his strengths lay

*outside the day-to-day running of the business, and he did
not want to be someone who was kicked upstairs.*

*We came to my father with a succession plan, including
a time horizon for implementation and his initial reaction
was "What about me?" This was definitely not something
we had anticipated! My father was in his late 60s, but now
it seemed that the position of honorary chair was not going
to be interesting enough for him. In effect, our whole succession plan became totally derailed.*

Fraser felt that going back to square one in the succession planning process was not an option, and he expressed an interest in
leaving the family business.

*A few months after this bombshell, I went to my father and
made it known I had lots of opportunities elsewhere and I
was thinking of departing the family business. My brothers
knew how unhappy I was and told me to come up with a
time horizon for leaving, and I informed my Dad I would
be moving on.*

It was at this point that the company's five-person Voting Trust
came into play. Three of the five persons were non-family senior
executives with the firm.

My father went to each of the voting trustees and told them that I would be leaving. They replied that my father could afford to lose my other two brothers, but he could not afford to lose me and they would vote against my father. Reluctantly, my father came back to me and promised to step down in a few months if I would change my mind and agree to stay on. I remember him saying, "Is my hand-shake good enough for you?" and I replied, "Of course, as my father, your handshake is good enough for me." In retrospect, what I should have borne in mind was one of my father's favourite sayings, "Divide and conquer," which was always his strategy when faced with more than one opponent.

What transpired next came about when Alex didn't like the way things were shaping up and got advice from an esteemed business friend. Alex went out and bought the voting shares that my uncle's family owned, and then he went to my father and asked what it would take to buy his votes temporarily so he could break the voting trust. My father came up with a list of demands; Alex agreed and got the necessary votes. Dad contacted me and said, "Your brother has taken over, and you and Ian are out in the cold," or words to that effect. To say I was shocked is an understatement.

These events transpired over the summer holiday season which added to Fraser's difficulties.

There was a board meeting called to ratify the vote, but because it was during the holidays many of the board members who would have supported me were away and out of reach. I even had to scramble to get adequate legal representation. I was able to put in a buy/sell agreement that was in favour of my older brother, but afforded me an opportunity to exit. We implemented a shotgun clause as well. I tend to think of the shotgun agreement as similar to there being one piece of chocolate cake left and two people wanting the last piece. Whoever cuts, the other person chooses. Essentially you try to do it so that you are comfortable whether you are on the buying or the selling side. In our case, it was Alex who was the buyer and Ian and I who were the sellers.

Fraser's older brother had gone to extraordinary lengths to gain control of the family firm, and this story has a less than happy ending.

When it came to crunch time, my brother's lack of business education and experience proved to be his downfall. Within three years, he ran the business into the ground. So, as a family, we were not successful in transitioning the business to the third generation. I think that to a certain extent, a family business is like a farm. You're not taking much out when you are working there, but its value is gradually growing. Essentially, you're a steward passing it on to the next beneficiaries. However, when you step away and take your share with you, you are undermining the basic structure to some degree.

After an emotional roller-coaster ride, Fraser was finally free of any association with the family firm and able to move on.

First off, I'd have to say that exiting the family business made me very glad that I'm married to a psychologist. Also, I'd learned from other families in business that if you are going to get bought out, then do it right away. Don't let the buyout occur over time. Leaving a business is not a simple matter – there's a lot of emotion, history and tradition involved. I'd spent a lot of time agonizing over what I should do. It was kind of a relief when it was all over. The downside, of course, is that we were not able to maintain friendly family relations during this experience and there are scars that will probably never heal.

Looking back, I'm pretty sure that because of the way we were brought up, we would have ended up fighting, no matter what. If we had grown up with a different family dynamic, where working together was promoted, then things may have come to a different ending. The only way to avoid what happened in our case would have been to divide the family business.

Despite the unfortunate turn of events that saw him ousted from the family business, Fraser has been successful in forging a new career for himself.

I basically look at things from a positive perspective. I cashed out at a terrific time so, personally, it was a very profitable way to leave. I've gone back to my first passion and have now established a merchant banking business. I only choose to work with people I like and respect, and that was not the case when I was working with my brother.

The other big plus has been quality of life. I'm under a lot less stress now and enjoy having much more time to spend with my wife and our kids.

At this point in Fraser's life, he is also somewhat philosophical about the role of a good owner.

If you are a good owner, you put together a governance structure and hire the best people. The chances of you being the best person to run the firm are actually not that high. You can play an important role on the strategic side, but don't try to be the best person. You can't be everything to everyone. The most important thing you need to identify is what is most important to you and go with that.

As for the future, Fraser has no sense of building his new business to pass on to his children.

The last thing that I would want is for our children to inherit too much and do too little. Of course, I am happy to help them out a little along on the way. When it comes right down to it, "Don't live for the business, live for the family."

WHAT THE ADVISERS SAY

Fraser McFarlane witnessed a difficult demise of his family's business. His story is a painful reminder that personal relationships alone cannot always be relied upon in a family business. Without the protection of legal documents, Fraser and his brother Ian had little control over their destiny.

Coming from a family that had been defined by its business for two generations, Fraser had felt obliged to enter the firm along with his two brothers. Although their working relations were not always smooth, the critical problem was their father's inability to let go of the reins. A situation developed in which Fraser and his brother Ian were left no choice but to exit the business.

The McFarlane case is a perfect example of what happens when there is no formalized succession plan. In this instance, Fraser and his brothers had overcome personal differences to arrive at a compromise only to have their efforts derailed by the intransigence of their father. With a strong advisory board in place, there is a chance this situation might have been prevented.

LESSONS LEARNED

- **Importance of communication**

  Good communication is key to the development and implementation of successful succession plans. Families frequently experience communication breakdowns when they are so involved with the business that they don't have time to step back and reflect. Had the McFarlanes operated their business on the basis of shared values and principles, the potential for conflict would have been minimized, and any disagreements would have been mediated by approved resolution mechanisms or in an appropriate forum such as a family council meeting. Formal agreements among the family members would likely have prevented this unfortunate outcome.

- **Need for stewardship**

  Had there been guidance earlier on in the career development paths of Fraser and his brothers, the impasse they ultimately reached may have been avoided. By making a successor development plan, the brothers could have mapped out and prepared for their different roles in the business. As Fraser points out, each brother had unique strengths and skills to devote to the business. Ideally, a plan for each brother would have been drawn up and presented in a family council meeting, thereby allowing for transparency in the family governance.

- **Keeping priorities in mind**

For many years, Fraser found himself being all-consumed by the dynamics of his family business. After he was forced out, he benefited enormously from a less stressful life and an ability to devote much more time to his wife and family. Fortunately, he was able to walk away from a bad experience with both his wealth and values in tact and is now able to pursue a rewarding career.

There can be enormous pressure on successors to put the family business first. But careful consideration should be given to other important priorities. In this particular situation, Fraser is actively involved in instilling values and a work ethic in his children and helping them to come up with values and priorities for their own lives.

BROTHERLY DIFFERENCES

· · · · ·

Paul Gorlach and his brother Daniel operate one of the largest marble and stone importers and distributors in the Toronto metropolitan region. The company was founded in 1950 by their father John who immigrated to Canada from Russia after years of experience working with the family-owned Gorlach Quarry in Suzdal.

In its infancy, John's business concentrated primarily on servicing the funeral monument trade, but by the time his sons Paul and Daniel came on board, Gorlach Stone was also a leading supplier to both the commercial and residential markets. With the demand for high-end finishes in residential applications showing no signs of diminishing, the owners are considering the launch of a comprehensive kitchen and bathroom design service.

Of John's four children, only Paul, 65, and Daniel, 63, are actively involved in the family business. While the two brothers have spent years working together, they have radically different views on family business succession. Four of John's 13 grandchildren are currently working for Gorlach Stone, and the hope is that they will jointly take the firm to the next level. Paul believes the way to do this is to challenge them to demonstrate their initiative, but Daniel is extremely reluctant to relinquish control or even discuss any aspect of the business transition. Paul finds his brother's position extremely frustrating and has brought in a facilitator to help find a way through this impasse.

> *Currently, my brother and I run the business together. He loves the day-to-day operations and the control. My role is more to monitor and advise, but we make all the major decisions jointly. Daniel, my two sisters and I own the company equally. We have no formal board. Our inactive siblings never challenge what we do and, other than our basic salary, everything is split four ways. I guess the potential is always there for conflict, but if you have transparency and the ability to communicate to other family members, then it can be okay.*

While Paul has always worked hard to ensure the success of the business, he also acknowledges that there are many other factors at play.

As a family business owner, two jobs have to be done – you have to run the business and you have to keep the family together. If you don't keep the family together, sooner or later the business will end up being sold.

It is important for me to see the business stay in the family – first and foremost because it's a business that was started by my father, and I think he always envisioned it being kept as a family business. Second, I think all of the family members will be better off, financially and otherwise, if we keep the business in the family. Say we sold the business and wrote everyone a cheque – that could work for them, or it could work against them. I really believe that keeping the business in the family means keeping the family whole.

Paul sees being engaged in the succession planning process as the way to ensure that the business stays in the family, but Daniel disagrees.

My brother's reluctance to even participate in the succession process is a huge impediment. He has no confidence in the next generation and no willingness to allow them to make mistakes. He has this need to control. In my opinion, control is for managers, not leaders. He is constantly questioning why we are planning for succession. He wonders why we are even talking to employees and gaining their input.

My brother thinks he will never exit, and that's a huge part of the problem. I can see that in the next couple of years the young ones coming up are going to get more confident, and they are going to be less tolerant of his need to control everything they do. Sooner or later, they're going to say, "Get out of the way." This kind of issue could divide our families and force us to sell. This is why I am being proactive with our succession planning – if we do it right, the business will remain in the family.

Unlike his brother, Paul has given a good deal of thought to his own exit strategy and what he hopes to achieve before he leaves.

The way I look at it, no man on his deathbed ever said, "I wish I had spent more time at the office." My exit plan is that I am going to be here for five more years, and each year I will take less of an active role. I see myself as being avail-able for consultation – don't expect me to identify or solve problems, but by all means use me as a sounding board. At our last family council meeting, I announced that I would only be working another five years. They did not react posi-tively or negatively, rather they just accepted my decision as a reality, and I appreciated that.

I believe leaving a legacy is important. I think the world should know that we contributed and made a stamp on history. Before I leave, I would like to see us have some cause that we support on a regular basis directly out of our proceeds – a cause that serves people with medical, financial, psychological or emotional problems. We need to settle on a cause that the whole family can feel good about supporting.

While Paul has come to terms with his own retirement plans, he realizes that a great deal of work remains to be done in transitioning the business to the next generation.

We have four children from the third generation working in the business. Whether or not there is an ultimate leader for the firm in that group has yet to be determined. At the present time, I have given the four of them a month to come up with a five-year strategic plan for our business. To tell you the truth, I am not really concerned about what they say in the business plan. It's more of an exercise to see if the four can work together and co-operate on this project. If it turns out that they can't work together, then this will tell us the only way succession will work is if we appoint a leader.

My brother, of course, has never been very supportive of this exercise, but I see it as a valuable learning tool in many ways. It will force the next generation to learn as much as they can from current management, and it will also be a signal to management that sooner or later they will be accountable to a different generation.

While Paul is giving all four members of the next generation the opportunity to succeed, he believes that his own son would be best suited to take over the running of the company.

Without wanting to sound biased, I know that my son has the ability to lead our business. He is the appropriate age and has had experience working outside the family business, which none of his cousins have had. I think the person who leads this business has to have outside experience because it provides you with a measure of your own self-worth. As a leader, you have to know that you are leading the business because you are capable and not because of your last name. And the same goes for the people who work for you.

Paul himself worked for a number of years outside the family business, and he sees this as another point of separation with his brother.

My brother Daniel has not worked anywhere else a day in his life. Ever since he graduated from university, he has been in the business. And as I said to the third generation, this is not a good idea, as you don't have the confidence. I don't care how smart you really are or how smart you think you are, you just don't have the confidence in yourself to trust other people unless you have broad experience. And what do we have in business other than people?

Paul is greatly challenged by his brother's reluctance to commit to succession planning, but he is still motivated to keeping the business in the family.

There are some days when I get really frustrated and feel like saying, "Just write me a cheque, and I'm out of here." We'd be lost if it weren't for the fact that we hired a facilitator – right now he's the glue that's keeping everything together.

We've had a number of family council meetings, and I'm hoping that my brother won't stay in denial. Neither of us will live forever, and we have to make plans. Personally, I wouldn't have a problem if none of the next generation took over and we hired external management to operate the business, but the thing is, as shareholders, we would still need to oversee them.

We were all brought up to be fairly modest – people in our family don't have to have public attention because of how much they own. There is no need to go out and do something just because someone else did it. The way our business is run now is very informal and based totally on mutual trust. I think as long as those types of attitudes prevail, then our potential problems are minimized. But if those values change, then the next generation will have to deal with the ramifications.

WHAT THE ADVISERS SAY

The future direction of Gorlach Stone is hard to predict. Fortunately, Paul Gorlach has not let his brother's lack of engagement or the uncertainty over the next generation's succession prevent him from proceeding with the planning process.

The family is hedging its bets that one or more of the next generation will take over management. If it turns out that more than one individual assumes the leadership role, then the complicated issue of establishing a co-presidency will need to be addressed and suitable agreements put into place to resolve the inevitable disputes.

Paul displays an unusual degree of flexibility in envisaging the direction the company may take. Of course, his preference is to respect his father's wishes and keep the business in the family, but if that means creating conflict in the family, then Paul might make the decision to sell. This ability to look beyond the emotional ties affords Paul a perspective that is rare among business owners. His pragmatic approach is based on a recognition that the business could not succeed with the family in conflict or without clarity around leadership.

The size of the Gorlach family presents some particular challenges. To ensure transparency, it is essential that open communication be maintained with all stakeholders. This family has a number of active and non-active shareholders, which so far has not caused any problems. However, despite the fact that the inactive siblings do not currently challenge decisions made by their active brothers, that situation may change when the next generation takes over.

NEXT STEPS

- **Formalizing governance structures**

  There is a fair degree of informality in the governance of Gorlach Stone, so a top priority for the successful transition to the next generation is to establish rules regarding issues such as decision-making. As well, the family council could be used more strategically to settle contentious issues.

- **Establishment of a phased retirement plan**

  A gradual, staged retirement plan should be established for each of the Gorlach brothers. The next generation can certainly benefit from their mentoring, but it can get complicated when a company has two active generations of executives working together for an extended period of time. Expectations and lines of reporting should be clarified and employees of the company should be made aware of the transition.

- **Creation of a private foundation**

  A good way to involve and unite both active and non-active members of the family would be through a philanthropic venture. Paul has already expressed a desire to move in this direction, and setting up and operating a private foundation could provide a focus for the family. This would help preserve the family's legacy, regardless of whether or not the business is sold. It would also require family members to work together towards shared goals and would provide Paul and Daniel with a second career during retirement.

'ONE STEAK A DAY'

· · · · ·

Arnold Rosenberg started his working career as a systems engineer at a time when computer mainframes took up an entire floor of an office building. Feeling somewhat constrained by the civil service bureaucracy in which he worked, Arnold took an idea he had for software development and set up his own business.

From his office base in Ottawa, Arnold's fledgling firm has grown to be a major developer and distributor of educational and scientific software with an international customer base. At this time, Arnold, 61, continues to enjoy the day-to-day management of his company, but he is looking ahead to the possibilities offered by retirement.

You look in the mirror and you see a little grey hair and real-ize that you might not be around forever. A couple of years ago, I started playing around with the idea of going back to school and getting a doctorate. That started the thought process of how things are going to go with the business when I am not around.

Many people in my position are looking to their kids to carry on the family legacy, but I've always thought that puts an unfair burden on the next generation. In my case, my son has got a great position at the bank and my daughter has her own family law practice. If they want to become involved with the business, it should be entirely their decision.

Never one to procrastinate, Arnold decided to set the wheels in motion and seek advice on how to restructure the company to effectively transition the assets to the next generation.

Of course, the name of the game is to minimize the tax implications – I worked with my advisers to achieve that and also give my kids the flexibility to do what they want in the future. They're perfectly capable of picking their own advisers when the time comes.

As far as our operations are concerned, we now have a holding company with four or five subsidiaries. Essentially, what I have done is convert the principal assets of the business to negotiable securities, and then all of that was transferred into a new holding company. The new company is owned 50–50 by the two kids. They have no votes, but technically have all the financial benefits. It is essentially more of an investment portfolio than anything else.

The bottom line is that if I kick the bucket tomorrow, I have already given everything away so the tax implications for my estate are not there. My children will eventually pay taxes when they take the money out of the corporation.

Arnold takes a philosophical view about the future of the business he has worked so hard to establish.

The day-to-day operations depend on the creativity and the ability of the individuals who work at the firm. It would be up to the kids to decide if they want to come into the business. At this point, it doesn't suit the goals of either of them.

If they continue to feel it is not for them, then they will need to decide on a CEO and what equity one should give or sell to an individual to continue the operation. I have no concerns about my children making these decisions together. They have the wherewithal, and I have given them recommendations about whom they should speak to for advice.

Arnold has tended to apply the same systematic approach to retirement as he would to the solution of a programming problem.

I've often thought of my father's words regarding retirement.

His point was we put a lot of effort into getting trained and prepared for our careers, especially if you're a trained professional like a doctor or a lawyer, but very few people put the same time and effort into planning their retirement.

In my own case, it was important to me to take care of all the legal, financial and tax aspects of transitioning the business. So I got myself some good advisers and took advantage of their training. We went through all the necessary steps and ticked all the boxes. At the time, it did take quite a bit of effort, but now I have the freedom to consider my options and my kids have the freedom to choose what kind of role they would like to play.

When it comes to the specifics of how Arnold will actually spend his retirement, the answer is less clearcut.

I still get a lot of satisfaction from what I'm doing with the business and find the research and development side interesting and challenging, so it's quite possible they're going to end up having to carry me out.

One thing I don't have is a fear or concern over not having something to do. I definitely want to become more involved in the community. When I do have the time and am footloose and fancy-free, I will certainly get involved in some sort of community charitable effort. I don't mean involved in the sense of writing a cheque, but rather being constructive in a low-key way. Perhaps, I could get a group of friends together and we could take on a project, doing what is required and maybe using what influence I have – that's something I would really enjoy doing.

Arnold would be the first to acknowledge that he is becoming more philosophical the closer to retirement he gets.

I take the view, like a farmer, that "one doesn't own the land, but one borrows the land from the next generation," so whatever you've created, you have created to add to the next generation.

And when it comes to building up your assets, you reach a point where you realize you can only eat one steak a day. It's a matter of being realistic – we only have a certain number of days, and we should make the best of those days by doing what we enjoy, having fun and sharing the pleasure.

As far as my estate planning is concerned, I have some assets set aside. I'm by no means a Bill Gates or a Warren Buffett, but I have specified which charities will receive distributions upon my death. These will be anonymous donations – I have no interest in being known for my good deeds, but I feel there are certain charities that are deserving of my money. I suppose this is all part of my philosophy –

only eat one steak a day, share what you have created and enjoyed, and leave your mark in some small way.

WHAT THE ADVISERS SAY

Arnold brings an excellent perspective to retirement and exit planning. He has established a structure that allows his children the flexibility to make career and business operating decisions at their discretion.

Despite the fact that he has not decided when he will officially leave, he has taken the time to recognize that he could put his time and intellect into rewarding initiatives when he is retired.

If, as seems likely, Arnold's children choose not to assume an active role in the business, then the business may be sold, resulting in liquid assets. The children will need to decide if they wish to pool these funds and manage them jointly or each go his or her own way to manage their share of these assets.

NEXT STEPS

- **Development of a share-option plan**

  Talent is the critical bloodline in a software business. Regardless of the role the children play in the business, consideration should be given to a share-option plan to attract and/or retain talented employees. Arnold needs to decide on the percentage of ownership he is willing to give up through share option dilution and then create achievable performance incentives that trigger the options. The challenge will be to strike a balance between providing employees with incentives while still retaining control.

- **Anticipation of conflict**

  Arnold is assuming that just because his children get along now, they will continue to get along in the future. This is a common mistake in estate and succession planning where parents find it difficult to be objective about how children will manage conflict. The ideal mechanism for conflict resolution is a pre-defined process that utilizes the help of third-party mediators.

- **Creation of a private foundation**

  As suggested for other families, Arnold would benefit from creating a private foundation to be the focus of his career during retirement. One of Arnold's primary goals is tax minimization, and establishing a private foundation is a tax-efficient mechanism to achieve philanthropic goals, especially in a year of a business disposition. By managing the foundation and working on different philanthropic initiatives in an organized manner, Arnold would have an outlet for his creative drive, fulfilling his desire to "leave a mark."

FINAL WORDS

· · · · ·

Through the generosity of business families who have shared their thoughts and stories, we begin to see why so many families struggle with succession planning.

Emotions often override reason when a family faces the transition of a family business, and the so-called "soft issues" usually take precedence over technical challenges such as creating the most tax-effective strategy.

Certain issues are common to many family stories:

- How to raise children to be stewards of wealth while at the same time avoiding issues of entitlement and nepotism.
- Working with family members who have completely different visions for the future of the business, and different views on the effectiveness of management.

- Communicating effectively with the family in a manner that manages conflict.
- Addressing the conflict between an owner's dream of passing on the business to the next generation and the children's desire to fulfill their sometimes competing aspirations.
- Dealing with siblings who each have a sense of entitlement, yet possess talents, skills and experience that may be inadequate.
- Handling family dynamics when children marry, have children of their own, separate or divorce.
- Facing and adapting to market changes and economic slowdowns.

The challenge of dealing with these difficult issues prevents many family business owners from establishing a successful succession plan. However, this is an achievable goal for any family so long as the proper supports are in place.

To encourage families to take the first steps towards a successful business transition, BMO Harris Private Banking offers a manageable approach to the succession planning process. We help our clients work through three essential steps:

1. Goal setting
2. Strategic planning
3. Implementation and exit

While every client needs to work through these steps, our approach is tailored to the unique circumstances of your family business. At BMO Harris Private Banking, we begin by seeking a full understanding of your personal situation, and only then suggest succession planning tools appropriate to your needs. After a thorough analysis, the planning process is broken down into manageable and measurable steps, and many options and resources are provided to assist you in the successful transfer of your business.

I. GOAL SETTING

This initial step forms the critical foundation for all that is to follow. We assist you in the process of determining your core values and goals. To do this, we ask your family to consider a number of questions: Are you committed to keeping the business in the family? Do you wish to sell the business? Do you wish to take a "wait-and-see" approach to keeping the business in the family?

Some of the questions are best answered if you have looked into the future as well as into your past. Your personal vision helps you to answer some fundamental questions such as where do you see the business in five years? Where do you see yourself in 10 years? What role does your family wish to play in the transition or sale of your business?

If your goal is to keep your business in the family, then we recommend turning the succession process into a family affair. Create an environment that fosters open communication and engages the next generation. Work together on plans, solutions and decision-making, ideally through family meetings using an objective facilitator who can help develop the essential skills for family communication. If part of the family's vision is to keep the business in the family, then the following are suggested courses of action for developing family governance with the help of your succession adviser:

- Craft a mission statement defining how the family wants to work together in the business.
- Establish a Family Council to provide a forum for family meetings. It is important to include family members and spouses of family members who are both active and inactive in the business. The Family Council will also provide a forum to educate and update family members on current challenges and plans for the business.
- Educate family members on ownership, stewardship and wealth-preservation issues.
- Resolve not only the question of ownership, but also the leadership and management of the company.
- Create family employment and development plans that outline appropriate compensation for family members working in the business.

2. STRATEGIC PLANNING

Once the goals are determined and the ground rules have been established, the next phase requires taking a step back and using your advisers to help determine *how* to meet your goals from both a business and family perspective.

Our focus at this stage is to work with the family to ensure continuity of the business during the transitioning process. We assist business owners in devising a methodology to analyze the business as an entity, separate from family and management concerns. A Strengths, Weaknesses, Opportunities and Threats (SWOT) analysis of your business is undertaken that assesses the size and complexity of the business in addition to determining the business needs from a leadership point of view to ensure long-term viability.

Once the needs of the business – as distinct from family or shareholder concerns – are fully understood, the qualities required of a successor begin to emerge. If family transition is contemplated, then a succession development plan for a potential successor will be created, defining the gaps that need to be filled in terms of both formal and informal education and detailing the experience that needs to be obtained from both inside and outside the business. Once in place, it is important that the successor development plan be monitored by a non-family mentor who is able to evaluate progress and establish a timeline for meeting pre-determined goals.

3. IMPLEMENTATION AND EXIT

Once goals and a strategy are set, the family will have a clear direction about the future of the business, including whether it is to be kept in the family or sold to an outside party.

Regardless of whether the decision is to sell or to keep the business in the family, it is important to communicate and stick with the succession plan that has been created.

Typically, a succession plan will consist of the family's mission for its business, the shareholders' agreement, the family participation plan, the business continuity plan, the successor development plan and the estate plan, including any philanthropic goals.

Ideally, the implementation of these plans leads to a well-managed and phased exit strategy for you, the retiring business owner. Communicating with employees and customers regarding the succession plan is crucial. Employees will be grateful for the opportunity to be "in the know" at the appropriate time and will likely be more loyal to the business during the transition if they feel a part of the process. It is the air of uncertainty in some family business successions that has a demoralizing effect on employees. Customers and suppliers will also appreciate being advised of the proposed change in leadership.

Should the decision be made to sell the business, you will need to work with advisers on determining its value in addition to creating a desired timeline for its sale and your exit.

Given the complex issues and emotional upheaval that often

characterize a family transition, it is not surprising that many families choose to sell instead. However, planning the sale requires a great deal of attention and work, and can be a distraction from day-to-day operations.

Apart from maximizing after-tax sale proceeds, other considerations such as confidentiality, timing and ease of execution are common issues that affect the way a family chooses to market and sell their family business.

There are families who attempt to sell their businesses without the help of their advisers or an intermediary. This do-it-yourself approach can have a negative effect on the value of the business and the stability of key employees and is, therefore, generally not advisable. Emotions experienced during the negotiation process often cloud good business judgement. It is always better to take advantage of the objectivity of experienced professionals.

Regardless of whether the business is sold or transferred within the family, owners are encouraged to set aside some time for retirement planning. Without a plan in place, many owners find the challenge of no longer being actively involved in the business difficult to bear. In these cases, a great deal of confusion and conflict can occur between the departed owner and the succeeding generation. For this reason, retiring owners are strongly encouraged to engage in a phased-exit plan, after which they may look forward to achieving their personal retirement goals, including travel and possibly philanthropic initiatives.

In this final phase of implementing the succession plan, a key consideration is the financial security of the exiting business owner. A family business that can afford to cash out the owner has a huge advantage over the situation where the departing owner is dependent on the continued profitability of the business, and liquidity is frequently an issue. However, creative planning can find ways around this problem.

While effective succession planning is challenging, the good news is that we know from experience that a positive outcome is possible. The hard part is getting started, but with help from our knowledgeable professionals and experienced advisers, you will be clearly up to the challenge.

GLOSSARY

· · · · ·

ADVISORY BOARD

A board acting in an advisory capacity to a family or family business. Typically, members are drawn from outside the family and have expertise in the areas of tax and estate planning, investment management, accounting and tax compliance. It is the role of the advisory board to provide objective advice on managing the business and developing and implementing a succession plan.

BENEFICIARY

The recipient of assets dispensed through a will or trust.

BOARD OF DIRECTORS

The role of a board of directors is to advise management on how to preserve the corporate assets for the shareholders while seeking an adequate return on investment. The board can be made up of officers and/or shareholders of the company, as well as individuals who are external to the company.

BUSINESS VALUATION

A formal assessment of the value of a business using pre-determined and generally agreed upon formulas. The discounted cash-flow model is an example of a frequently used method.

BUY-SELL AGREEMENT

A legal document providing for the transfer of ownership of a withdrawing partner's interest in a business. The agreement spells out the conditions under which the buyout can take place and typically specifies a pre-determined valuation method.

COMMUNITY FOUNDATION

A community foundation is a locally run public foundation that pools the charitable givings of many donors. Its mandate is to build and manage endowment funds to support charitable activities in a local area.

CONTINGENCY PLAN

A plan designed to minimize disruption to a business in the case of a sudden departure of leadership due to disability or death. A contingency plan seeks to provide for interim leadership and the successful continuation of operations until a succession plan can be implemented.

DISPUTE RESOLUTION PROCESS

A mechanism for managing and resolving conflict using a process to which all parties have previously agreed.

DONOR-ADVISED FUNDS

A form of charitable giving whereby funds donated to a public foundation are directed to the charities of the donor's choice. This form of directed giving provides a cost-efficient alternative to the creation of a private foundation since responsibility for the administration and management of the funds is assumed by an organization established for this purpose.

EMPLOYMENT POLICY

A policy created by the family that clearly establishes the rules and expectations relating to the employment of family members. Such a policy will contain provisions regarding hiring, role definition, compensation, promotion, accountability and termination of family employees.

ESTATE FREEZE

An estate freeze fixes the value of the owner's equity in the business at its fair market value so that any future growth accrues to the benefit of the children or other designated beneficiaries selected by the person implementing the freeze. In most cases, the estate owner exchanges assets, usually common stock, for fixed-value preferred shares. New common shares are then issued, usually for a nominal consideration, to the beneficiaries or to a family trust established for their benefit. Usually, the preferred shares are redeemable at the option of the holder for a price equal to the fair market value of the shares for which they were exchanged.

FAIR MARKET VALUE

The price that a willing buyer pays to a willing seller when they are dealing at arm's length in a free market.

FAMILY COUNCIL

A family council provides an organized forum for family members to meet and discuss the current and future state of the family business. Members may, or may not, be directly involved in the day-to-day business operations. The family council is a way of building family unity and cohesiveness through a shared vision of the family's guiding principles. These principles are sometimes given formal expression in a family mission statement.

FAMILY MISSION STATEMENT

A family mission statement is a communal expression of a family's values, ethics, and goals as they relate to the current and future operation of its business and the legacy it wishes to create.

INCAPACITY

The state in which a person is no longer able to manage his or her affairs due to a physical or mental disability.

INDEPENDENT DIRECTORS

Members of a board who are neither family members nor officers of the operating business.

MEDIATION

A non-adversarial approach to conflict resolution by which a neutral third party (the mediator) works to facilitate the settling of a dispute between two or more parties.

NEPOTISM

Showing favouritism to family members without regard to merit.

PLANNED GIVING

Planned giving is a means of leaving a legacy. The donor commits to a direct gift to a specific charity in a process that maximizes tax and other financial benefits. A gift can take the form of cash, stocks and other investment instruments, life insurance, works of art, land, or other assets, and can be made during the donor's lifetime or upon death.

POWER OF ATTORNEY FOR THE MANAGEMENT OF PROPERTY

A power of attorney is a document that names a person or corporation to act as a substitute decision-maker regarding an individual's financial affairs in the event he/she becomes unable to make decisions for various reasons, including incapacity.

PRIVATE FOUNDATIONS

An organization whose sole purpose is to support charitable endeavours, primarily through the distribution of grants. Normally created by an individual or a